A Secret Life

First published in 2021 by Blue Diode Press
30 Lochend Road
Leith
Edinburgh EH6 8BS
www.bluediode.co.uk

ISBN: 978-1-9164051-6-5

Thanks to the Czech Republic Ministry of Culture for a
grant towards the production of this book.

MINISTRY OF CULTURE
CZECH REPUBLIC

Typesetting: Rob A. Mackenzie.
text in Pilgrim LT Roman.

Cover art, design, and typography: Emily Chappell.
Diode logo design: Sam and Ian Alexander.

Printed and bound by Imprint Digital, Exeter, UK.
https://digital.imprint.co.uk

A Secret Life

Milan Děžinský
translated by Nathan Fields

Blue Diode Press
Edinburgh

Contents

3. Roots and Stalks –

4. Whisper in the Opera

Acknowledgements

Thanks to the editors of the following publications
where several of these poems in translation have been
published:

BODY
The Dark Horse
Lyrikline
Modern Poetry in Translation
PN Review

Thanks to Host Publishing in the Czech Republic
for permission to publish these translations, to Jan
Zikmund of the Czech Literary Centre in Prague, and
also to Joshua Mensch and Justin Quinn.

Sieve

They attentively sifted their whole life through a sieve.
They believed something would remain and not fall through,
but their names will fade,
the sun whitens them, the wind grinds, the rain washes away,
neither in memories, nor on damp paper,
and I know, not even in poems,
let alone in poems.

1

Laugh in the Rain

I'll Be Thirty-Three

They leave me alone
and while the kettle clucks like a hen,
I realize that at my age
Ginsberg and Corso had long written
the most beautiful poems:
about a girl from Park Avenue,
about thought, which is all
the poet knows of death.
Even I am sometimes seized by an itch
that cannot be relieved until one
slumps down into transformation,
as if an ugly flower were struggling up out of one's chest
and *someone else* were plucking the petals,
but it was as if they were tearing out a wart,
something revoltingly yours,
penetrated by fate,
veined with spongy tissue,
expressing itself with sweat,
which is a manifestation of craving
but also of openness
when I address myself in a whisper
here at this lamp, here in this darkness –

By the Fire

First the dog disappears
and for just a second leaves a tail of flame behind it.
Then the boy takes away the last light in the lantern
and gets lost in Oort's Cloud.
I'll stay a while longer with the numb Neolithic hunters,
that whisper with embers. Their narrative deepens the pit
I fell through so that I could surface where
I left myself.
The ashes dim.
Living things freeze
and those eternally still move gently.

Waking Up

All I know is that this is waking up.
Warmed by a trickle of water in the gutter,
leaning against the membrane of a throbbing vein. Black power
rises up. I'm searching still half-blind
for a shaken-off shoe.
The dark places where I feel good hold me by a handle of bone.
Dreams slipping like clothes out of a hotel closet
are flowing into my awakening
like blood into a wound.
I perceive a mere melody of thoughts.
But now I'm starting to look around.
I finally see my benevolent room,
I feel the damp bed
and monstrous banality.

Celebration

When I spotted the dead guy I felt like when
they bring you in and take the blindfold off your eyes.
Today I recall his glossy face.
Funereal guests, serious and aware of the moment,
bow over the polystyrene complexion
and over clasped palms, like when you knead to grey
all the clay. The room is dark;
light inspires unceremonious thoughts.
Mourning is an orderly expression of grieving.
They watch slightly askance so as not to be struck by
    the discharge
of some kind of posthumous prescience that might flare
    up out of the matter.
The dead guy had been carefully groomed and prepared.
I only wondered at how still he lay there
in view of the seriousness of the celebration.

Atom

It is sixty-five years since Hiroshima,
they write. Should one cup a handful of water from a river,
there is certainly in it at least one atom of oxygen
that Cleopatra exhaled, I have read,
or was it Marilyn?
I hear my daughter's sobbing
through the wall, in whose marlstone joints
still trembles a tear of builder's sweat.
The house is secreting saliva from the bedrock.
When she struggled her way into the world,
I paced the room.
Had she been given a gift
of one atom from Hiroshima?

Buzzard

I had taken him to his mother
and was returning along the D8.
In the breakdown lane several cars, and behind them
scattered papers like a snail's track.
I thought about how many things
it is possible to learn: to speak again, to use your legs
instead of your hands, to let yourself like a newt
grow joy inside your body,
tissue to tissue, joyfully linked cells.
Like a table cleared with a sleeve, the empty highway
signaled that the healing time
would be written with a tiny pinkish scar
into the calendar of memory.

And then – I saw it out of the corner of my eye,
like someone indicating an attack
and a shadow passed perilously
like a startled doe –
a falling buzzard, rotating, like when a plane's engine
cuts out, and then crashes
into the azure highway
somewhere far behind the car.
I imagine that disheveled remnant,
collapsed into itself upon the merciless surface,
as if it still didn't know how to fly,
chilled in her meager nest
and she watched that blue above her,
predatory head adamantly lodged
between two wings whose tips
are ruffled by the breeze like a promise...
I watch behind me as her bird body
calms in quivers, the wind ruffling her again
as it slowly dissolves
like sleep.

Burrow

September starts, brushing over your neck with its fox tail,
you sit with your back to an open door, a door
to the long corridors of an empty house,
these corridors continue on and turn into a forest
with an underground burrow in which anything can happen,
and anxiety wheezes through the very forest, those corridors,
from the burrow within which anything can happen.

TV Star

The smooth armpit of a TV star
explodes bluely in a solitude of darkness
and you're stuck, eaten
like a shoe caught between two
continents sliding against each
other,
you crumble with the mobility of a clod,
like when you saw those lovers' hands
in the shopping centre,
two hot, collapsing,
centripetal universes
curved
towards good moments
and the unrepeatable
shabbiness of the day.

The Tarnished Shine of Alpaca and Silver

It points to the good old times
that remain misunderstood.
The clock ticks and it's difficult to keep pace with it
in this tired hour. Old poets
encourage the soul, but dry out the hands.
The lamp in the kitchen forever in the same place.
You search for a reference to your own life,
but you're looking along the walls.
The signal faded in the light.
It's still possible to sleep.
You are already walking slumber's edge,
where boulders creep upon boulders,
underwater sounds are heard,
but only fish can see them.

State of War

In the uncovered slope of overturned layers,
like when a foot is long stifled in a tight shoe:
A concertina of *Carboniferous, Triassic, Permian* – shuffled
    cards.
The dull stone skull of a cynodont juts from one of them.
Beside the tracks above the river, swans have armed
    explosives under their wings.
You reach an end that disappears like a flare in a gun barrel.
In the blackness men buried beneath a mound
of snoring. You look back nervously under covering fire.
In a window, beside a flower pot,
someone has set a celery's fuse.

Memory of the Dormitory

You walk along the bank and wool warms your ears.
A coal boat approaches and an owl hoots.
I'm coming back from nowhere
and in the distance I see your wedding gesture to the swans.

I remember how you got up that time
and walked out to the vending machine in the hall.
You never came back.
Did you fall into a paradise of salad bowls
at a laid table, a purgatory of morning papers
and removed shoes? A hell of kitchen appliances?

1985

When she ironed,
it smelled of starch and canvas,
in the choral of that aroma Sunday stiffened,
tidying was done, and when someone said war, they meant
that war...
but the wall seems impossible to scale only when we are
a step away from it, the wall... But we didn't often think
about the war. On Sunday we watched
ski jumping on TV.

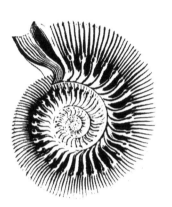

2

Outlet and Gullet

Sparrowhawk

I would like to have a woman's empathy.
What do they think about when they're shaving?
It's stopped raining. I'm looking out into the yard,
above which a bird is fitfully circling.
I looked in the encyclopedia.
I have never seen a sparrowhaw;
It suddenly struck me that I would die
without ever having seen a sparrowhawk,
or worse still –
I'd die while chewing something –
or otherwise ridiculously –
with one foot in a pant leg –

I Am

The whim of cause and effect has allowed
us to dwell in a favourable fate
with which nothing remains but to disagree
and simply suffer it. The fascination that the usefulness
of the brightest star is a trifle
compared to even the warily wriggling embryo
of a thought. As if a microbe were hatching
that has both the power to kill and alluring mucous
within its bursting core.

And so I sit here in a tangle of my memory
bound to the present and I am only by the fact
that I am.
Nothing more. I accept warmth from the cloth I am
wrapped in.
So frightened by the fact I am. Like a bone
which knows it is more than a bone –
that it trails with it the tale of lime.

Halley's Comet

No revolution is in progress,
it's just our mysterious future
creeping in from somewhere.
It emerges from an archeology of shadows
and taps in time.
Through the wall I hear an old woman
welcoming a squeaking door.
She looks down the street
like through a telescope,
but sees only the back of a stranger.
She knows what's not awaiting her,
but has no clue what awaits her.
When Halley's Comet
flies over, we'll be together.
struggling up out of the soil,
changing into leaves,
golden pollen will whirl
branches will be bent
so she can see it.

What if...

Everything stops.
A bewildered silence seizes up within the veins of plants.
Your arm looks long for the light at the end of the sleeve,
where the future is safe,
where anxiety is definitive
and nothing comes after,
time takes on its cautious stiffness,
half a cat juts threateningly from around the corner,
my sentence to you is cut off in the middle of the message,
only it doesn't plunge from the precipice like a desperate
    body,
your gaze towards me seems like a too slowly pushed-off
stocking, but nothing comes after,
nothing comes after...

Having Iceland

To Iva

Just to be self-seeding, alluvium,
to have your own Iceland.
Uncultivated fields of heather,
from west to north.
To have you there,
a cold-irradiated, clear being
even a lost, improper thing,
because you love the tropics, a hot sea,
into which you would know how to sink
like a streak of light that slips
into the entrails when someone tries to speak
in a solitary moment.
And then at night dresses torn from hangers,
just to have dresses torn from hangers,
crumpled like faces on the plains.
To have your future and hold it, too, as
wonder and understanding that something is.
That something simply is.
Long ago the same as far away
on your borrowed plains.
Just to have your own future
and dresses torn from hangers;
to be alluvium and self-seeding
to have your own island
to have your own Iceland.

What to say about a world

that stands out where it's not smooth.
To disappear in the fields and never return.
Let a messenger ring
and not leave a message.
To walk out to the edge of the forest.
Change into a tree in front of mushroom pickers,
and stick out oddly in the shade, so that they notice,
with a root knotting the footpath.
Be whipped like a dog rough with a rope.
Let the boy rustle the branch with a stick.
Be the resting place
of a sparrowhawk zeroing in on a dove.
Stand bare against Alpine wind,
have in your bast an ingrown message
that remained undelivered.

Story

Everything roughens and a body beneath a sheet
perpetually shivers. That's a story,
turned into a tiny round whole.

It would be.

Were there not a knee so coldly protruding from it.

Words Have Meaning

Words have meaning,
even if we say this and that is beautiful,
women are gorgeous;
the frost of dawn biting into
the dry stalks of birds' nesting places
has its chilling beauty.
The story borne by a wrinkle
on a face in a train compartment, scenes from alien worlds.
That we will never know what happened to those
we passed on the street just like that,
they live their own secret lives in other places
and speak with such ordinary beauty
about the dead, dresses and children.
Spring's haberdashery is naturally beautiful in a way,
perhaps even from a deer stand, in the crosshairs of a rigid
    hunter.
And being on an *actual* watch is beautiful,
when the moon rises and the calf of a homeless man shines
from under a bridge.
We do not think of what will be after death
unless there is something after it.

Mollusc Shells

As if in an endeavor
to leave something here,
but I don't have in mind kilos of soft tissue.
It's as if I were in a wormhole:
I change the channel and see that same face,
just cast roughly by time:
young Annie from Trautenberk
and the schoolteacher from better times,
all those black-and-white fairy tales
full of the living dead.
It's like a collection of mollusc shells
rattling in a shoebox.
Is life long or short?
There are plenty of other things
to think about,
what to eat and what to wear,
dispelling feelings of loneliness,
there even remains a moment for compassion,
love, and white lies.
Someday everything will rattle
in another box.

Into the Darkness

Return to the darkness, Ranchetti calls out
from one of his poems, as if he were still wavering,
to see whether there were another way. But there's not
from the moment we were
waterlilies in the womb and wrenched
by a random, undesired gust.
And so it *goes* on.
We unconsciously search for an outlet
or a gullet, depending on whether it's just
getting rid of us, or swallowing us;
we wake in the night,
when in our sleep we're frightened by a deer,
with steam rising from its back,
which is getting up out of the snow heavily
on three legs.

3

Roots and Stalks –

* * *

You remain and all else goes,
you flee from whatever stays,
and come back, like Apollinaire,
like a figure without a face,

to the place that still persists
chained to wood you lie on
and gently repel the wood
and hug yourself with iron.

Spring

Benumbed bees on partially open
blossoms like detaching fingernails.
Bracket fungus dusts the spring moisture
like musty flour.
The observant face of Theodore Roethke
hatches in a chicken wrinkle.
The air smells of memory.
A grub beneath a sandal
digs a black hole in a parallel universe.
Jolting its translucent core.
The past has found a crevice, the world rejoices.
Just before noon
a plow dislocates a rat head from the soil.

Forest Party

Stones retch into the chilly night
and wrinkly chanterelles shine through blueberry bushes.
Here the fragrance of fruiting bodies flies
on male strength. Wood moistens with desire,
ferns stiffly scroll their tentacles.
A nearby dwelling does not squander its light.
There's no room for memories.
In a rotten stump with standing water,
dreams hatch like mosquitoes
and are discharged onto the city
in an aerial duster.
Amanitas rub each other with cold
like translucent penises.
Movement in a burrow.
A viper goes cold around a root.
A dormouse tunes and pulls out its instrument.
The Central Bohemian Uplands bear fruit!

Cutting

Cutting into bread, defiant in its acquiescence.
Cutting into a pepper crunches menacingly like the bolt of
    a rifle.
Cutting into a potato with a starchy stutter,
like when a zipper starts to open and the line of the cut fills
    with blue.
A careless slit in a wooden tabletop is a wrinkle.
Cutting inspiring a thought or movement.
The mechanical cutting into a rabbit to remove its head
holds grace in the snap of the spine.
The sharp cutting into a mushroom, smooth as butter cake,
strikes the whole forest.

Whim

A trick of boredom from which no work arises,
just the last pocket of resistance,
like when a dry, ravaged tree
seeps one final vertigo of sap upon an old ant
that couldn't muster the strength to escape.
This is the most ridiculous whim:
that a bloated second,
in its moment of hunger,
changes what will be once and for all
a dead-motionless floating island,
sinking into the shadows.

Jewellery Box

The earth flourishes through frost, a snowdrop of veins
penetrates deeper, transforms water, strengthens quartz.
A grub morphs into a gem and bursts.
At night the frost attacks in force
and diamond worms explode underground.

Orderly Existence

A tree rots in the forest unnoticed.
Lichen trims bark. A raucous reek.
The bruised framework sinks into the earth.
A woman with a man's physique treads the path sobbing.
The night telephone above the table takes a bite out of
    the darkness.
A dog that begins to howl in its sleep,
as if it weren't supposed to be alive anymore.
Power over words is power over things.
We sleep and have everything – relations,
a favorite restaurant, happy home.
But something here's not clicking. Not only words.

November

Such a picture of withering
demands active engagement.
Chrysanthemums bloom into the snow
like the colour of a wounded animal.
A free moment between increments
of time filled with decay.
The mathematical beauty of frost.
Structures organize.
The end of struggling through mud.
At the end of November the plum tree
smells like dog kibble.
We sit and watch the chickadees in the feeder,
drinking hot tea, a celebration of security
with dusk's familiar arrival.
Who wouldn't love the grey Sunday afternoon;
we're already so far from the scene with the fox
dragging its injured spine along the highway
like stolen prey.

Burning the Branches

After winter my loved ones burn branches.
Children listlessly suck deadnettle flowers.
The sweetness saturates this day in May.
Reeds are burning. A blackbird chick flits
from a dog with a cry.
An insect melts above the fire.
A lizard is a twisted, rusty wire.
Birch above the flames flutters and raises dust
like a broom.
A hedgehog flees, on his back a burn-fused scab
of spikes. We look into the fire,
as if again witnessing
the creation of the world.

Jigsaw

I stop at the wall of the moist forest:

A log drowns in mud like a deer halfway up its chest.
Silence buzzes after crickets.
The extinguished star of a snail shell
whose light swallows me
and then spits me out a bit further.

At the footpath a jigsaw.
Two birds' scattered skeletons
mingled in one last turtledove kiss.

They will lie there, I imagine,
in that beautiful forest,
in rain, in heat,
chill,

till new birth
does them part.

4

Whisper in the Opera

Hunter

I.

The power,
when a poem is not created, but comes into being,
when it settles in grooves like a tree ring in the furniture,
it creaks and in its quivering disturbs
the peace of the dust.
Like a hunter, I wait for this moment
rubbing a numbed leg.
Spring dawns above the wing of the forest,
the hunter cools his cheek against the gun barrel,
which will, any moment,
certainly turn into an antler.

II.

I have a metaphor in mind,
large and complicated,
when from my morning bowl of muesli I
clumsily fish out a precious
hazelnut,
it's burrowing all the way to the bottom.
I, vigilant hunter,
will find it in the end.
That effort is rewarded with delight,
though what's left is a lot of muesli
and no hazelnuts.

Tomatoes

Yellow and rusty layer of leaves
peel like old skin,
light sprays along houses, cars, fences
pours over a greyish face in the window – it's me,
life behind me, another life before it
in a series of small movements.
This moment is only a delay:
tomatoes,
waiting blankly at the executioner's block,
on the verge of exploding and sourly burning
the impression of morning, scorch the light,
burn the face.
Victorious tomatoes.

Accessory

I wouldn't be able to love her.
Just the suspicion of that giant tongue…
But when she spoke she skillfully concealed it within the hollow
from which darkness spews.
Crimson, dully shining accessory of mortality.
But I knew it was there, filling her entirely,
that perhaps as a living muscle it had devoured
the space of her body along with her organs. A fleshy slithering
  parasite.
Although everything was forcing me to believe it was only my
overactive imagination, I knew it was there.

* * *

Based on the poems of John Donne and Allen Ginsberg

It so happens that before you fall even deeper
below the rustling thirst of leaves, loose soil,
through the chasm of memory before awakening,
you will fall in like a puzzle piece
among the mingled bones of lovers,
between his fragile metatarsals
and her white femur.
Taut in frozen horror,
witness to their endless intercourse,
you won't move, for fear of being caught.

Among Debris

Every secluded corner will one day be a square in the
    metropolis.
All life will be discovered and all death clarified.
Hills and forests will be disassembled in the dark of night
and placed into boxes and reassembled just before dawn
and arranged along the highways.
The calm before the storm will become the storm before the
    endless calm,
from which you will poke things through a slot to the other side
there, where you lived.

A Secret Life

The thought that a secret life really exists
is terrifying. Shadows would dress for the night
and set out into the rain. While sleepers are experiencing
    dreams,
they steal off towards the lamps stark naked under coats.
But maybe it's just part of the plan –
all those cloaking manoeuvres, obligations, stupor and sex,
for a secret life can only be played out in sharp light.
We have but unreliable evidence: a bitten nail,
strangely coloured flakes of skin, a fragment of a poem on a wall.
An unseeing vein bit its way through a muscle.
Very bright side light colliding with muffled music
is like flushing.
A forgotten or exchanged object. A watch in the fridge among
    the eggs.
Or –
The secret life is the visible part – property issues,
getting up for work, parental effort, the need to share,
gruelling weekend fun.

Things

To look closely
at the soft things coiled into branches
clinging childlike,
without explanation,
things of concealed birth, nocturnal fertility
too high above the floodplain,
too insignificant for divine intervention –

and elsewhere, out on the highway, a ragged, crimson shirt,
tattered by the wind, seams laid bare by water,
a few hairs still glint in it,
as if a guy had rakishly unbuttoned it at his throat,
washed out to the edge of the ordinary,
cars slow down and speed up again,
steering clear of it,
or when the child in back
wants to know the name of a predator.

Gravitation

They're having a picnic, but it looks as
if they were taking the tools out of the car in an emergency,
or they are taking the tools out of the car,
but it looks as if they were going out on a picnic.
A body does not thrust itself against the floor of an elevator,
but the elevator against the body.
Dusk does not fall upon the city,
the city slides creeping in beneath the dusk.
A hawk does not propel itself towards a mouse,
the mouse catapults itself against the predator.
At the opposite bank a barge rolls the river under itself.
We are not approaching our end,
but from ultimate emptiness
the end is hurtling towards us.

Lovers

As if they were trying to pull each other down
under the sharp edge of the waterline, where voracious demons
stretch out their hands from their underwater empire.
And having the upper hand. Pushing him below you:
The fierceness of bones, the voracity of membranes. One
    emerges:
using his last strength to breathe, a tuft of hair devours his palm,
leveraging with a knee. Buttocks beating with the heart of a
    horse.
So as in times long ago, even today
passionate, deadly aggressors. And when everything is over,
the shudder slowly fades in the pectoral girdle.
The heart is quiet. They are each alone.

Long Dim Days

They open a box of rum-filled pralines.
The pralines are going grey.
Heavy curtains shake the must.
They move the chairs throughout the morning.
The floor creaks to a televised
conversation. Desire changes into dinner.
Joy is a sweet prize, a cake,
A blanket slides down the slope of an ancient couch.
The doorbell's glare at times tears through the darkness of
    the room.
They're mustering the courage to approach the window.
A hand draws back the drapes. The cornice piercing rattles.
A grey and blue creek of coats
flows around umbrellas.
Their eyes pick out kids'
raincoats of orange, pink and green
like jellybeans.
No mail today.

Tuareg

Based on the experience of Z. Štolovský

People on the street
emerge unawares like divers.

When two Tuareg meet, however,
they come alive and already start greeting each other from
    a great distance.
When they meet face to face, they rub palm against palm,
they ask about family, sheep, camels,
neglecting nothing.

Great, fanning gesture.

When they part, they wish a safe journey,
and as they gradually move away from one another,
they still chat a little,
like when there's a bit of tea left at the bottom.

Then, slowly shrinking,
they quiver and fade against the horizon,
like a well being filled.